# OTT/CTV
# PROGRAMMATIC
# ADVERTISING
# GLOSSARY

---

**+ 150 OTT/CTV TERMS** RELATED TO ADVERTISING, BUSINESS, DEVICES, SERVICES & TECHNOLOGY

GW00730508

*:tappx*

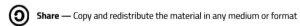

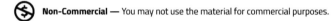
© Tappcelerator Media SI, 2021

**Drafting:** David Lahoz, Héctor Rodriguez
**Cover design and layout:** Javier Sánchez
**Composition** (for printing): Mariana Eguaras
**Translation:** Jay Pereira

Tappx is a registered trademark of Tappcelerator Media SL

# INDEX

Tecnology

 Services

 Devices

 Advertising

 Business

## 4K  Technology

Ultra-high definition video. We refer to 4K when the screen has 4,000 horizontal pixels.

## Ad Exchange  Advertising

Technology platform where programmatic advertising transactions are carried out connecting demand (DSP; demand side platforms) and supply (SSP; supply side platforms).

## Ad Network  Advertising

Advertising platform where inventory of different publishers, who share a direct contractual relationship, is sold.

## Ad Server  Advertising

Technology that allows advertising to be served on digital media, facilitating the segmentation of campaigns. The system keeps statistics of the results generated by the actions as well, favouring their analysis and optimization. There are two main types of Ad servers: Support, in charge of serving the campaigns in the publisher, prioritizing them according to the publisher's business priorities. Agency, which facilitates the monitoring of the campaigns served by the publishers' Ad servers, making it possible to break up data, and measures the effects of the campaigns on the digital properties of the advertisers.

## Addressable Advertising  Advertising

TV advertising model that allows, through the same content, to personalize the impact on households thanks to the execution of different advertising campaigns depending on the profile of each household.

## Ads.txt / AppAds.txt  Advertising

Text file that the publisher locates in its properties (support website or of the publisher of a mobile app) which lists the companies with which the publisher has direct agreements to sell its advertising inventory in the programmatic ecosystem. This tool brings transparency to a highly automated marketplace and helps prevent fraud.

## Advanced Video Coding (AVC)

Technology

Advanced video compression format. Also known as JVT, H.264 and MPEG4 part 10.

## Agency Trading Desk

Advertising

Team within media agencies or advertisers in charge of managing the purchase of programmatic advertising campaigns for their clients through the use of one or more DSPs, and which are segmented with data that can be activated from DMPs.

## AI (Artificial Intelligence)

Technology

Machine learning model that allows programs to simulate the human learning model. In the video market, this model is used to generate content recommendations, follow user activity within the platform, and generate metadata through audiovisual content.

## Amazon Fire Stick / Amazon Fire TV

Devices

Device developed by AMAZON that, when connected to a television set allows downloading APPs and accessing video platforms, games and digital services through the Internet.

## Android TV

Devices

Version of the ANDROID operating system designed to be used on televisions and decoders. Companies interested in it must be certified by Google before being allowed use it.

## AOSP

Technology

AOSP stands for Android Open Source Project, an independent initiative that facilitates the development of the Android mobile platform. Unlike Android TV, this free version allows device manufacturers to change anything they might they consider important

## API

Technology

Application programming interface. One of its most relevant characteristics is to enable your software to connect with others, facilitating the interaction between them.

### App spoofing
Advertising

An ad fraud scheme in which a malicious party impersonates another application, causing the ads to redirect to applications that mimic other more popular apps.

### App Store
Services

Market that enables companies to offer, for free or with payment models, downloadable applications for users. An example is the iOS, Google Play and Roku app stores, etc.

### Apple TV
Devices

Apple device that, when connected to a television, allows users to download applications and watch videos over the Internet.

### ARPU
Advertising

Stands for Average Revenue Per User. This metric indicates how much the viewer spends on the services of an operator during a given period, thus making it easier to analyze and plan the profitability of an IPTV / OTT service.

### ARR
Business

Stands for Annual Recurring Revenue. This metric indicates the amount of money that a company generates per year through its business model.

### Aspect ratio
Technology

Ratio of width to height of a screen. The NTSC standard uses a 4: 3 ratio that is closest to a square, and HD televisions most often use a 16: 9 wide format.

### Automated Guaranteed
Advertising

Automated advertising transaction in the private market where an advertiser buys placements at a fixed price for a limited period of time. It is the variant most similar to purchasing traditional non-programmatic media.

### AVOD
Business

Advertising Video On Demand is the name given to the video on demand service that generates income by playing advertisements within the service.

An example is the free YouTube platform, which plays ads over its videos and has display ad placements with which it generates revenue.

## Bandwidth
Technology

Bandwidth is the volume of data that can be transmitted from one point to another in a fixed period of time. Depending on the type of online service, different bandwidths are required. For example, in a standard definition (SD) video (480p) this indicator is set at 1 megabit per second (Mbps), while in high definition (HD) videos (720p) it is raised to 4 Mbps.

## Binge-watching
Business

A common practice among OTT video platform users of watching episodes of a web series back to back until the available content of that series is finished.

## Bitrate
Technology

Bitrate is the compression ratio of the video data transmitted by the source. The higher the bit rate, the better the video quality.

## Bit-rate Management
Technology

The speed at which data is transferred from one point to another is defined by its bit rate. Bit rate can indicate the quality of an audio or video file. With bitrate management, your streaming content is adapted according to the connection capacity available on the end user's network.

## Cable TV
Technology

Traditional model of transmission of linear television services through a coaxial cable. Cable channels can also be used to provide Internet access, video on demand services, or voice services.

## Catch up
Technology

Technology that makes it possible to access digital content through the Internet at a time after it is viewed on a linear television channel. This is thanks to it being possible to record high-quality content in real time, which makes it easier to reproduce it later at the user's request.

## CDN (Content Delivery Network) Technology

Network of servers located in countries that serve the content according to the location of the users. It is used to optimize the loading speed and guarantee the optimal experience for the end user.

## Chromecast Devices

Google Set-up box that connects to television sets and allows the downloading of applications to receive audiovisual content over the Internet.

## Chromecast built-in Technology

Technology that enables the user to enjoy their favorite shows, entertainment and applications on their television or speakers using their mobile device, computer or tablet as a remote control.

## Closed Captioning Technology

Transcription of the dialogue in the audio channel of a video that is reproduced simultaneously with said video.

## Cloud Video Distribution Technology

System where video files are stored on online servers, which makes it possible to access and view them from anywhere. This fact optimizes the experience of the end user. Cloud Video Distribution systems can be used as another name for CDNs (Content Delivery Network).

## CMS Technology

Content Management System. System used for the creation and publication of digital content. Its applications range from creating web pages to inserting images, graphics or videos into them.

## Co-Viewing Business

Traditional television term that is also used in connected television. Audience meters try to estimate how many people watch traditional television, even when a group of people are simultaneously watching the same television. These estimates allow advertisers to pay for every person who might be viewing their ads. In the case of digital video services, the user is referred to as the person who is consuming a service, that is, who is viewing a video, although there is no unified response in the market. It is expected that in the future there will be a unification in the audience measurement models of the different platforms, thus allowing all audiovisual consumption models to follow the same parameters.

## Cookie Technology 

Files sent by a server to a web browser that are stored on the hard drives of users' devices. These files allow the collection of information about the user's browsing activities on the website that created the cookie.

## Cord-Cutting Business 

User that switches from a paid cable television subscription to an Internet television (OTT) service. In other words, part of the market that goes from traditional pay TV models to new OTT platforms.

## Cord-Nevers Business 

Users who never paid for a TV subscription, but who do consume OTT video services.

## Cost Per View (CPV) Advertising 

Name given to the cost per reproduction of an advertising video when a predefined minimum viewing time is reached. There are other billing models for advertising videos such as the cost per full view (CPCV; paid only when the video is seen to the end) and the cost per visible video (CPVV, where it is paid only if the video is visible according to the standard, meaning that the video occupies at least 50% of the number of visible pixels for at least 2 consecutive seconds).

## CPM Advertising 

Stands for cost per thousand impressions. The cost that an advertiser must pay for 1000 ads to be served.

## Cross-Screen Measurement Advertising 

Monitoring and measurement of video metrics on mobile devices, tablets, digital outdoor advertising, linear television, Smart TV or computers where an attempt is made to identify the net audiences that have been exposed to content or advertising, regardless of the device where it has been consumed.

## CTV

Business

Connected TV refers to devices that use a television as a screen and connect to the Internet to access audiovisual content.

## DAI (Dynamic Ad Insertion)

Advertising

Ability to exchange an ad in a linear television program for an online spot. This solution works on video on demand services.

## DEAL ID

Advertising

Tag that allows to identify an agreement between buyers and sellers in the programmatic ecosystem. For example, buyers can purchase inventory at defined prices on a private exchange that may not be available to other bidders.

## Device farms

Advertising

Advertising fraud in which activity is repeatedly generated on a device in order to simulate legitimate use, resulting in an illegitimate advertising demand.

## Device spoofing

Advertising

An ad fraud scheme in which a party maliciously impersonates another device. An example would be device emulators making ad requests.

## Digital television

Technology

Transmission of television and audio images by encoding video and audio to digital formats. It mainly uses the MPEG data compression standard. However, depending on the area of application, there are several standards:

**DVB-T** - which is the European standard for digital television.

**ATSC** - The American digital television standard.

**ISDB**: the Japanese standard for digital television.

**DTMB**: the Chinese standard for digital television.

## DMA (Designated Market Area)

Business

Designation of specific geographic markets that are often classified according to population size.

## DMP  Advertising

Stands for Data Management Platform. Centralized data management platform that makes it possible to determine audiences by following a combination of data from various sources (navigation, advertising campaigns, CRM), own and / or third parties. The DMP, along with programmatic buying and selling platforms (DSP and SSP), allows these segments to be inserted into advertising calls in order to segment campaigns.

## Dolby Digital Plus  Technology

Multichannel digital audio storage and transport compression scheme. It is also known as Enhanced AC-3 (DD +, E-AC-3 or EC-3).

## DRM (Digital Rights Management)  Technology

Business model and technological platform that allows the protection of intellectual property online and the property of videos or other content. This makes it possible to retain ownership of the content and prevents illegal distribution or access.

## DSP  Advertising

Stands for Demand Side Platform. Technological system that makes it easier for programmatic digital advertising buyers to carry out automated campaigns on different aggregated traffic sources and segment them with data from different sources. In addition, it favors automatic optimization depending on campaign results.

## DTC (Direct to Consumer)  Business

When the content distributor does not need intermediaries to get their product to the final consumer. For example, Netflix does not require a television channel to show its content; delivered DTC.

## Electronic Sell-Through  Business

Online audiovisual content purchase model. Allows users to download and own a copy of the video. It is the model on which TVOD (Transactional Video on Demand) is based on.

### Encoding
Technology

Process by which data is converted to a particular format to facilitate its transmission and storage.

### EPG
Technology

Stands for Electronic Program Guide. Software with an interface where the platform user can access the different available content (linear and on demand) through enriched descriptions.

### FAST
Business

Free TV broadcast services with advertising, that is, they offer free content that would otherwise normally be paid content.

### First Price Auction
Advertising

Programmatic auction in which the winner pays the price offered for the impression in the bid.

### First-Party Data
Advertising

Data obtained in digital sites and / or CRM of our property. They are considered of higher quality since the holder has the makeup of how the different audience segments have been created.

### Floor Price
Advertising

Minimum price, set by the publisher, for which the inventory can be sold.

### Framerate (fps)
Technology

Rate of the speed of a frame, that is, the number of images (frames) contained in one second of video. When the human eye sees 10 to 12 consecutive images per second, it perceives the images individually, but when the number of frames is greater, the eye perceives the images as if they were moving. The NTSC system uses a frame rate of 29.97 fps and the PAL system of 25 fps.

### Frequency
Advertising

Number of times a single user is exposed to a campaign. The frequency of exposure must be balanced to achieve the effect of memory of the message in the audience without saturating it through overexposure.

## FVOD

Business

Stands for Free video on Demand. Type of video on demand in which the subscriber receives unlimited access to videos without additional payment or display of ads.

## HbbTV

Technology

Hybrid Broadcast Broadband Television is the standard for displaying CE-HTML (Consumer Electronics HTML) web pages through a device. Often these pages contain additional information about the program being watched, such as sports scores, a related television slot, or a menu with access to other content. The HbbTV system also allows a television to be interactive since viewers can vote in real-time for a show's characters or participate in polls.

## HD (High Definition)

Technology

Stands for High Definition. Refers to any video with a resolution of 720p. However, it is generally identified with videos that are in a resolution of 1080i or 1080p. In such cases, one can speak of Full-HD.

## Header Bidding

Advertising

System that allows publishers to bypass the traditional cascade auction method, where demand / SSP partners are called in a predetermined order. Instead, Header Bidding enables publishers to organize unified auctions in which all bidding partners compete simultaneously in real time.

## HEVC

Technology

Stands for High Efficiency Video Coding. Video compression format that converts high-quality video files into others with their size reduced by half but maintaining image quality without notable alterations.

## HLS

Technology

HLS or HTTP Live Streaming is the most efficient method to broadcast live over the Internet. It divides the feed into smaller packages, which enables efficient delivery.

## HTML5 Technology

Standard for configuring and presenting content on the World Wide Web.

## Hybrid Model Business

This model is linked to those OTT platforms that support a hybrid system of access to TVoD, SVoD and AVoD content for revenue generation.

## Impression Advertising

Metric used to count the advertising impacts generated in online campaigns that refers to the number of times an advertising piece has been served on the client device.

## In-Stream Video Ad Advertising

Ad played before, during or after the transmission of video content that the consumer has requested (pre-roll, mid-roll or post-roll). These ads generally cannot be paused or skipped while viewing.

## Intelligent OTT Technology

OTT service that uses artificial intelligence to follow the consumption of users and, using this knowledge, makes suggestions based on their habits.

## IPTV Services

Stands for Internet Protocol Television, a blanket term referring to online audiovisual services.

## ITU Business

The ITU, which stands for the International Telecommunication Union, is a global organization that was established for the purpose of standardizing and regulating international telecommunications and radio. Its powers include the establishment of interconnection agreements between different countries.

## KPI Business

Key Performance Indicator. General term that refers to measures of the success of a company. Among its indicators is the its revenue growth, participation in the market or the growth of its customer base.

## Linear TV

Technology

The linear TV nomenclature refers to traditional television services. That is, the model in which programs are transmitted over the air using systems such as digital terrestrial television or a satellite connection.

## Live Stream

Technology

Live streaming video in real time that is distributed over the Internet.

## Metadata

Technology

Content metadata refers to various properties (information) of a content, such as title, description, story, cast, promo image, trailer, etc.

## Middleware

Technology

Middleware used to manage IPTV components. The operator requires middleware to control certain actions of the subscribers such as access to content, billing, allocation of service packages, etc.

## Midroll

Advertising

An advertisement in online video format that is played during a pause of the content, also in video format, being played.

## Mobile

Devices

Service through which the user accesses content through their smartphone or tablet. For this, it is necessary that the mobile device supports the functions required on the Internet. These services are normally distributed through applications developed for each of the existing mobile operating systems.

## Mobile App

Services

Stands for mobile application. Downloadable program designed for smartphones and / or tablets.

## MPEG

Technology

Stands for Moving Picture Experts Group. Group of specialists created by the international organization ISO to formulate standards in the compression and transmission of digital audio and video information.

### MPEG-DASH
Technology

Flexible bit rate transmission technique that enables the transfer of high quality multimedia content over the Internet.ExoPlayer."

### MRR
Business

MRR or Monthly Recurring Revenue is the metric that measures recurring monthly income.

### Multiscreen
Advertising

OTT operator service where the user can view digital content on one or more connected devices posses the installed software.

### MVPD
Services

Multichannel Video Programming Distributor. A service that provides users with a variety of television channels, such as cable or satellite television.

### OBS
Technology

Stands for Open Broadcast Software, a free, open source program that allows creators to record and stream videos. Created by the OBS Project.

### Online Video Business
Business

Nnline service that generates revenue selling access to its videos.

### Online Video Platform
Services

Platform that allows users to upload videos with the added possibility of generating revenue.

### Online Video Subscription Business
Business

Online video company that charges users a recurring fee for accessing its content. Also known as SVOD

### Open Auction
Advertising

Open auction where a publisher facilitates access to his inventory to all bidders connected through the SSP. The highest bidder wins the impression.

## Open Source

Technology

Free program or set of code for public use, and modification by developers.

## OTT (Over-the-Top)

Technology

Stands for "Over-the-Top". Refers to any traditional communication service that is transmitted over the Internet, as opposed to services with traditional video transmission cable or satellite.

## OTT App

Services

Application that enables users to consume videos online. Normally, these types of applications are available for different devices such as televisions, tablets, mobile phones, game consoles, etc..

## OTT Content

Technology

Stands for "Over the Top Content" which refers to video content that is transmitted over the Internet. This is in contrast to traditional cable or satellite video transmission.

## OTT Infrastructure

Technology

Physical and organizational elements necessary to operate an OTT service, such as internet connectivity, devices, screens, etc.

## OTT Platform

Services

Online service that allows users to access videos through applications or browsers on different types of devices connected to the Internet.

## OTT Streaming

Services

Video consumption over the Internet.

## OTT Streaming Service

Services

Company that provides access to videos that can be consumed online.

## Patreon

Services

A fundraising platform that allows content creators (including video creators) to share content with an exclusive group of subscribers.

### Pay-Per-View
Business

Video on demand service where users pay for the consumption of each video. Also known as TVOD

### Pay-TV
Business

Paid subscription television service.

### PiP
Technology

Stands for Picture in Picture. Technology for displaying two video images on a TV screen simultaneously. The main video image is displayed in full screen and the secondary video image in a smaller window.

### Place Shifting
Technology

Technology that enables any viewer with a broadband Internet connection to view television channels from their home television to the screen of any other device.

### Playback device
Devices

Electronic device that connects to the Internet using existing communication standards and technologies: wired (DSL, broadband, etc.) and wireless (Wi-Fi, 3G, 4G, LTE, etc.).

Playback devices include:

- Set-Top Box.
- PC.
- Smart TV.
- Smartphone.
- Tablet.

### Playstation
Devices

Game console manufactured by Sony capable of downloading OTT applications and streaming videos.

### Podcast
Services

Series of episodes made up of digital audio or video files that can be downloaded by a user for consumption.

## Podding / Ad Podding

Advertising

With the release of VAST 3.0, the concept of "ad groups" is introduced. This set must meet a series of specifications to be delivered sequentially. Podding is becoming increasingly important to publishers and media owners by providing a high-quality user experience on long-form video content. Podding offers publishers the ability to schedule multiple ads from a single request. These commercials will play sequentially, similar to a commercial break on linear television.

## Postroll

Advertising

Online video ad that plays immediately after finishing the video content being viewed.

## PPV Bundle

Business

Monetization feature on an OTT platform that allows you to select and watch a package of popular movies or series of a similar genre.

## Pre-Bid Targeting

Advertising

Data processing that allows advertisers to segment visible, fraud-proof, brand-safe, or context-relevant inventory and bid only for inventory that meets predefined requirements.

## Preferred Deal/Unreserved Fixed Rate

Advertising

Offer variant in the private market where a publisher or SSP offers inventory at a predefined price.

## Preroll

Advertising

Online video ad that plays before user-chosen video content is displayed.

## Private Auction

Advertising

Offer variant in the private market where the publisher selects a series of specific advertisers to participate in the bidding of their inventory, access being restricted to others.

### Private Marketplace (PMP)

Advertising

Higher value ad groups grouped by publisher or SSP and not available in an open auction. Only selected advertisers can bid on these placements.

### Programmatic Advertising

Advertising

System that automates the purchase of online advertising campaigns.

### Programmatic Direct

Advertising

A transaction between a publisher and an advertiser that takes place through a programmatic ad buying system. The inventory is sold and guaranteed directly.

### RAF (Roku Ad Framework)

Advertising

Advertising on Roku video platforms.

### Real Time Bidding (RTB)

Advertising

Real-time offer consisting of an offer request and a response to it. The offer request is triggered when a user visits a page. The request data (user location, browser history, website, device) is offered for sale through an SSP and an Ad Exchange. A DSP connected to this Ad Exchange responds to this offer with price and creative data (response to offer). The highest bid for the placement wins and the ad is served. All of this happens automatically and in milliseconds.

### ROI

Advertising

Return of investment. Shows the level of profitability or non-profitability of a campaign in relation to the investment made.

### Roku

Devices

OTT video streaming company that creates streaming devices and Smart TVs.

### RTMP

Technology

Stands for Real Time Messaging Protocol. System developed for the high performance transmission of audio, video and data over the Internet between

Flash-based platform technologies, such as Flash Player and Adobe AIR, and the server.

*Example*: A live broadcast can be transferred to the RTMP server and, via CDN and a compatible online video player, the broadcast is played back on user devices.

### SDK
Technology

SDK stands for Software Development Kit comes: Group of tools with which to create applications for a platform or language-specific coding.

### Second Price Auction
Advertising

Bidding model where the winner of the tender for ad impression pays one cent more than the second highest bidder.

### Second-Party Data
Advertising

Company-specific data that is purchased directly or through the synchronization of two DMPs.

### Set-Top Box
Devices

Physical device that connects to a TV screen and allows users to watch OTT videos on their TV.

### Smart TV
Devices

TV equipped with Internet connectivity, offering users access to OTT applications and video content without additional equipment.

### Smart TV Platform
Technology

Software that enables the operation of a Smart TV, such as Roku, iOS, Android TV and Fire TV.

### SSAI
Advertising

Server-side ad insertion, also known as "dynamic ad insertion." Method that makes it possible to insert advertisements into a video stream automatically from an external server.

### SSAI Infiltration
Advertising

Ad fraud scheme in which a malicious party forges IP addresses to impersonate real users, thereby attracting the expenditure of server-based ad placements.

### SSP
Advertising

Stands for Platform for the supply-side or Platform for the sell side. Technological platforms that allow OTT providers to manage their inventory of advertising space, incorporate advertisements and receive revenue.

### Streaming / Streaming On Demand
Technology

Type of audiovisual consumption in which users can immediately view content through the Internet, without previously downloading it.

### Subscription Business Model
Business

Business model based on subscription payments. Generally, the user pays a fee to access the content on a monthly basis.

### Subtitles
Technology

Transcription of the dialogue of a video that is played simultaneously with it.

### SVOD
Business

Stands for Subscription Video on Demand. Video on demand service in which a prior subscription is required to access the desired content.

### Teaser
Business

Brief fragment of an audiovisual product designed to awaken in users the need to see more or buy.

### Tech Tax
Advertising

Term used to define the costs applied for the use of technological solutions of the programmatic ecosystem. Among these fees are those applied for using SSP, Ad Exchange, DSP, DMP and the agencies' trading desks.

## Third-Party Data

Advertising

Aggregated data from platforms and data providers used to enrich programmatic campaigns.

## Time Shifting

Technology

Function of a video-on-demand service that allows the user to suspend viewing, pause or schedule playback for a specific moment.

## Trailer

Business

Short fragment of audiovisual content intended to promote it and thus attract users to see more or buy the advertised product or service.

## Transcoding

Technology

It is the process of adapting encoded digital files from one format to another in order to be able to reproduce their content on different devices.

## TV App

Services

Downloadable program from an application store, specially designed for viewing on smart televisions (Smart TV).

## TVOD

Business

Stands for Transaction video on Demand. Video on demand service where users pay for the consumption of each video.

## tvOS

Technology

Apple's native operating system for its Apple TV product line.

## User

Advertising

Anonymous or registered subscriber who accesses the content through a browser or software program by assigning a personal identifier that is registered in the operator's internal statistics system.

## VAST

Advertising

Universal XML script that allows ad servers to communicate relevant information to video players about the behavior of these ads on IPTV platforms. Among the information provided, you will find which ad should be reproduced, the format in which it is presented, for how long it is reproduced and if users have the option to skip it.

## Video Hosting
Technology

Web service that allows users to upload, view and share videos from their servers.

## Video Monetization
Business

The action of generating income from video content, whether through advertising marketing, subscription fees, paywalls or hybrid models.

## Video Subscription Service Platform
Technology

Service that allows the creation of a subscription video business.

## vMVPD
Services

Stands for Virtual Multichannel Video Programming Distributor. Service that offers users a variety of television channels over the Internet.

## VOD
Business

Stands for Video on Demand. System where users choose what programming to watch at any time. It differs from linear programming that traditional television carries.

## Voice Assistant
Devices

Application that allows verbal interaction in the user's native language. It can be used for setting alarms, calendar appointment reminders, controlling lights, music and other smart home devices, and of course making phone calls.

## VPAID
Advertising

Script that tells a video player which ad to play, the duration of the ad, when to show it, and where to place the play, pause, etc. actions..

## VTR
Advertising

Stands for View-Through Rate, i.e. the percentage of people who see a complete video or beyond a previously determined point. It is a metric that determines performance in digital video advertising campaigns.

## VTT
Technology

Stands for Video Text Tracks. Subtitling method that synchronizes video speed with text speed using timestamps. See also: Closed captions and subtitles

## Watch Time
Business

Period of time that the content is consumed by a user.

## Xbox
Devices

Internet-connected game console created by Microsoft that is capable of downloading OTT applications and streaming videos.

## XVID
Technology

MPEG-4 Part 2 video compression library based on the open source code of another codec: DivX.

## THIS GLOSSARY IS BROUGHT TO YOU BY TAPPX

Are you looking for a high-performance ad based monetization solution?
Contact us, we'd be happy to discuss about OTT & CTV monetization
and how we can boost your OTT Ad strategy, through our
exclusive AI-powered programmatic solutions.

**contact@tappx.com**

## About Tappx

Tappx is a fast-growth AdTech company that delivers digital advertising solutions for multiple platforms including mobile, OTT/CTV and desktop. Tappx's proprietary technology empowers publishers to maximize ad revenues across mobile and OTT channels. It offers a distinct point of difference – technology which has been specifically engineered for mobile and OTT markets, thereby offering brands and agencies increased trust and transparency. The Tappx platform currently processes over 20 billion ad requests per month worldwide.

# Contact

 **contact@tappx.com**

**www.tappx.com**

**www.linkedin.com/company/tappx/**

:tappx